I0446134

Obrist-isms

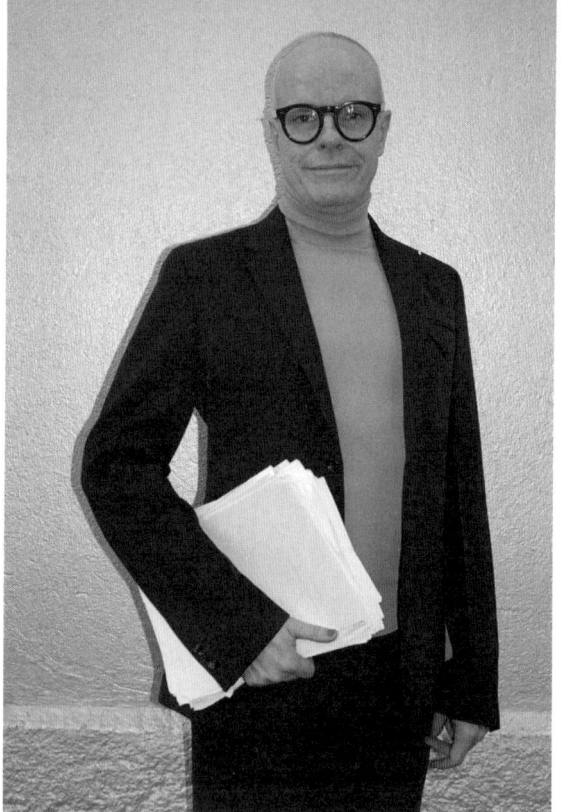

Obrist-isms

Hans Ulrich Obrist

Edited by Larry Warsh

PRINCETON UNIVERSITY PRESS
Princeton and Oxford

in association with
No More Rulers

Published by Princeton University Press,
41 William Street, Princeton, New Jersey 08540

In the United Kingdom: Princeton University Press,
99 Banbury Road, Oxford OX2 6JX
GPSR Authorized Representative: Easy Access System Europe -
Mustamäe tee 50, 10621 Tallinn, Estonia,
gpsr.requests@easproject.com

press.princeton.edu
in association with
No More Rulers
nomorerulers.com
ISMs is a trademark of No More Rulers, Inc.

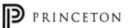

All Rights Reserved

ISBN 978-0-691-27984-8
Library of Congress Control Number: 2025936068

British Library Cataloging-in-Publication Data is available
This book has been composed in Joanna MT
Printed in China

1 3 5 7 9 10 8 6 4 2

CONTENTS

INTRODUCTION vii

Early Years 1

Curating and Exhibitions 19

Artists and Conversations 47

Archiving, Collecting, and Unrealized Projects 61

Édouard Glissant and Mondialité 77

On Sleep and Time 89

Art and the Environment 99

Technology and the Future of Art 115

SOURCES 131

CHRONOLOGY 143

ACKNOWLEDGMENTS 151

INTRODUCTION

Obsessive. Expansive. Connective. Reactive. These are just a few of the words that come to mind when I think of Hans Ulrich Obrist. A nonstop thinker who immerses himself in the minds of the artists he works with, Hans Ulrich has done much to redefine curating, transforming it into an art form in itself.

With great determination, he dove right in at an early age. From his groundbreaking first exhibition, *The Kitchen Show* (1991), Hans Ulrich has questioned where art is presented and how it's displayed. He breaks down the barriers to museumgoing. Although he continually works with outstanding institutions around the globe, he does not rely on the four walls of traditional exhibition spaces.

Instead, he finds inventive ways to redefine the relationship between artists and audiences, breaking old rules and improvising new ones. With a keen grasp of globalization and the interconnectedness of art, Hans Ulrich works to bring people together, share knowledge, and develop new avenues for storytelling. He understands how to look at art, how to listen, and how to disseminate the artist's mind. He knows language and storytelling. He is a lens through which we can see the creative process. Through his work, he makes others visible.

From the start of his career, Hans Ulrich has conducted a never-ending series of studio visits, soaking up the ideas around him like a sponge. He consumes art. He is a master archivist who makes knowledge accessible to all. He has embraced his role as a bridge builder in the art ecosystem, always asking how he can be useful to each artist and how to best convey the essence of their creativity. Curiosity is his engine.

Hans Ulrich is fascinated with technology and its applications to art, and he has a thorough understanding of this continually changing field and its implications for artists. He connects as easily with emerging artists as with established art world figures. He cares deeply about younger generations, and that concern for the future fuels his mission to "create togetherness and not separation." A generous mentor, he carries forward the lessons learned from his own mentors, amplifying an ongoing spirit of care, collaboration, and innovation. It matters to Hans Ulrich how he will be seen in a hundred or two hundred years, or frankly, how we all will be seen—and indeed whether we will be.

Hans Ulrich is a brilliant interviewer, conversationalist, thinker, and listener. Those are the qualities that, for me, come through most clearly in these pages. Gathering more than 250 quotes and excerpts, *Obrist-isms* offers an intimate glimpse into the creative processes of this deeply creative individual. Through his work, Hans Ulrich has done much to reshape the art world, producing a legacy that celebrates the boundless possibilities of creativity and connection. It's a pleasure and honor to have met him in my lifetime.

LARRY WARSH
NEW YORK CITY
JANUARY 2025

Early Years

I come from a family without any relation to the art world: my mother taught at primary school and my father worked as a controller.

(68)

———

When she was a primary school teacher, my mother encouraged her pupils to express themselves. She was sometimes criticized for departing too much from the rigid curriculum. This resonated with my interest in Ivan Illich—whom I never had the good fortune to meet. I don't suppose my mother was actually a disciple of Ivan Illich, but she was a kindred spirit. (3)

———

My mother was literary. She loved literature and she read huge amounts, especially [Franz] Kafka. She had a sort of hunger for knowledge. So she read what I sent her and was always asking me for more books. I sent her not just the books I had written, but also those I had contributed to. That soon became a lot, because I contributed more and more often to anthologies and group catalogues. And each time she read not just the small article I had written but the whole book. So gradually, after ten years or so, she began to know more and more about contemporary art! (3)

———

If you go back in time a little, in a way, you find the mother. When my mother died, something came full circle. (3)

———

When I look back at my early years in Switzerland, I find almost all the interests, themes, and obsessions that have shaped my entire trajectory appeared very early in a series of encounters with places and people: museums, libraries, exhibitions, curators, poets, playwrights and, most importantly, artists. (73)

———

Ever since my early adolescence, I've always written about art, I've never really made art. I mean, I'm doodling all the time, but that's just sort of thinking by doodling and sketching and all of that. (61)

———

When I was still in high school, I discovered this book by the great Alexander Dorner, *The Way Beyond Art*. It became a little bit of a manual to me. In it he describes that we can understand the forces at work in the visual arts only when we understand what's going on in other disciplines. (62)

———

When I was 14, I encountered the work of [Alberto] Giacometti. And that's the moment, really. It then became an obsession, maybe, with art and I started to look more and more. (61)

———

Something strange happened when I was 17. I went to see an exhibition by Claude Sandoz, a Swiss artist from Lucerne who was having a show in St. Gallen. And after seeing his work, which I got excited about, I went up to this person and said, "I want to meet the artist." And she said, "I can't really give you the number, but we can send him a letter." This was pre-email. So, they wrote him a letter and he received me in his studio, and it all went very quickly from there. (45)

———

I was born in the studio of [Peter] Fischli and [David] Weiss: that is where I decided I wanted to curate exhibitions, though I had been looking at artworks, collections, and exhibitions for most of my adolescence. (73)

From then it became a kind of addiction. I would obsessively visit artist studios. (45)

It was David [Weiss] who inspired me to set out on my own journey. He had gone on his long journey when he was young and I felt I needed to do the same thing. And so, for about five years, between '86 and '91, I didn't really produce anything. I just traveled, visited artists, and asked questions. (79)

I went by night trains because I couldn't
afford hotels—I would always try to go
to the next city at night. (79)

———

I'd do 60 cities in 60 days, by train.
It was a kind of European tour,
only very low budget. (45)

———

I would visit Alighiero Boetti in Rome,
Gerhard Richter or Rosemarie Trockel in
Cologne, Maria Lassnig in Vienna. Basically,
it became this nonstop studio visit. (45)

———

I was very inspired by the migratory monks, who learned everything they could in their monasteries and then would bring that knowledge to the next city. (48)

———

I was also inspired by this idea that one would carry knowledge to the next city, and then learn more; that after visiting hundreds of studios, I would also be able to share stories. (45)

This being the pre-mobile-phone era, night-train rides were also a kind of refuge from the world. I could reflect on what I had seen that day, make notes, and have conversations. Soaking up ideas like a sponge each day in the studios of artists I admired, I would process their work in my mind in the quiet of the train. (73)

———

So, in a way those early night train journeys very much defined the DNA of everything that would come later. (45)

———

None of my projects would have happened
without these five years of touring,
because it was a form of nurturing,
a sedimentation. (12)

———

My interest in interviews was first triggered
by two very long conversations that I read
when I was a student. One was between Pierre
Cabanne and Marcel Duchamp, and the other
between David Sylvester and Francis Bacon.
These books somehow brought me to art—
they were like oxygen, and were the first time
that the idea of an interview with an artist
as a medium became of interest to me. (80)

———

I knew that what I wanted to do in life was to work with artists, but I had yet to produce anything. I was searching for a way to make a contribution. What, in this art system, could be a first step, and above all, how could I be useful to artists? (73)

———

This idea of spending time, this idea of developing rituals, the exhibition as a ritual that creates connection, was for me important from the very beginning. So I organized this exhibition in my kitchen. It came out of a conversation with Christian Boltanski and Peter Fischli and David Weiss, independent of each other. They came to my flat and discovered, because I never cooked, that the fridge was completely empty, and the kitchen itself was full of books. ... So they actually made my kitchen into a real kitchen. In an interesting way that was the beginning, this production of reality. (27)

———

The idea was then that Peter Fischli and David Weiss would turn the kitchen into a kitchen with an exhibition, and they constructed this altar made of oversized groceries. (62)

———

Hans-Peter Feldmann used the fridge, making an exhibition within the exhibition. He did a fridge exhibition and showed marble eggs and feathers inside the refrigerator. (27)

———

Since this first experience I never stopped doing exhibitions in domestic environments and in smaller spaces. ... I think in a way the kitchen is always with me wherever I go. (27)

———

[Suzanne Pagé] asked me to write for her Giacometti catalog and interview all the artists who had known Alberto Giacometti, which was an amazing project for a 22-year-old curator to do because I could see Balthus, I could see [Roberto] Matta. I could go and see [Henri] Cartier-Bresson, Mario Merz, and Franz West. ... They were all still alive, these historic figures who knew Giacometti. Then basically I became part of the Musée d'Art Moderne. (7)

———

Suzanne realized that I was more like a free spirit. So she invented this *formula migrateur* for me, where little exhibitions could happen anywhere in the museum. (7)

———

My first meeting with Boetti was an epiphany for me, because he gave me a sense that there were still many unexplored horizons in working with artists. Through Boetti, I glimpsed the ways I might become a curator and still expand the field, still help to create newness. Not only did he instill in me the necessity of urgency, but my first ideas of what it still might be urgent to do. (76)

———

Boetti mentioned that it could also be a valuable thing for a young curator not only to work in a museum, a gallery, or a biennial, but to realize unrealized artists' projects. I think that was really the mission he gave me. (76)

————

The curator should just go and listen, really listen to what the artist wants to do, which might not be an exhibition—it might be something totally different. It might be a school, or a campaign, or. ... (37)

————

Artists gave me tasks, and I've done these tasks ever since. (45)

———

Curating and Exhibitions

[Curating] is much, much more than filling a space with objects. It has to do with filtering. It has to do with enabling, with synthesizing, with framing, also with remembering. (58)

———

When I was in high school in Switzerland, Joseph Beuys gave a lecture in which he talked about the arrival of his new concept of art, his expanded "Kunstbegriff." Inspired by that idea I thought to myself: If an artist is talking about an expanded notion of art, there should be an expanded notion of curating. (23)

———

What is happening outside the museum is just as important as what's happening inside. Make the walls porous. Think beyond exhibitions. Foster alliances. (40)

———

I am driven by curiosity; I want to understand how things evolve. (61)

———

The task of curating is to make junctions, to allow different elements to touch. You might describe it as the attempted pollination of culture, or a form of mapmaking that opens new routes through a city, a people, or a world. (73)

———

It's such a privilege to think of answers and to invent new rules with artists. That's something we cultivate as curators: somebody who will listen to the artists and then grow with the artists. (28)

———

I think the whole notion of a curator has to be permanently redefined. I think the ideal curator is the catalyst. (60)

———

Many great exhibitions have been curated by artists themselves. (61)

When one makes an exhibition, one invents
a new set of tools. (13)

———

My working process also entails making
unfinished exhibitions. They continue to
evolve and learn. (29)

———

A successful exhibition provides us with
extraordinary experiences, but also invents
and proposes a new rule of the game. (9)

———

The routine is the death of the exhibition, and I'm very much convinced that we need to redefine the necessity for every exhibition from scratch. (60)

———

Classic, traditional exhibitions emphasize order and stability. But in our own lives, in our social environments, we see fluctuations and instability, a plethora of choices, and limited predictability. (33)

———

Exhibitions should allow gaps, reversals, and strange collisions to be a vibrant location of permanent transformation. (33)

———

I think the best exhibitions make subtle arguments about history without falling into didacticism, and make links across history that go beyond mere decorative juxtaposition. (76)

———

The really relevant exhibitions are the exhibitions which have a historical necessity in that time: to be within one's own time, to be in the middle of things, but in the center of nothing. (65)

———

An exhibition can be a performative space, rather than a space of representation. (66)

———

We must always resist the tendency to
isolate art by imprisoning it in the gallery or
hiding it behind exorbitant admission fees.
If it is to be impactful, art should be made
available to the public, we must always
be driven by that principle. (23)

———

As a curator, it's my work to make
others visible. (52)

———

I believe in generosity as a medium. (28)

———

The revival of public art has been very strong. I have been writing during the lockdown about the Roosevelt plan and the whole idea of the New Deal. There was a lot of focus through that on public art, and we can see very clearly now that a lot of artists have the desire not only to do exhibitions but also to engage with longer-term projects in public art. (48)

———

Artworks are collected, but exhibitions are very often transient phenomena. ... There is the catalog, there is photography. ... It's the memory of those who saw it. (61)

———

In the 1990s, when I started working with my mentors Kasper König and Suzanne Pagé, we often had a year or two to organize an exhibition. The Broken Mirror was the first big show that I cocurated with König; it had an 18-month preparation period. But with the acceleration of art world schedules, I've been asked to do big shows three months out. You can't do that to artists, so I've often turned them down. (2)

———

It is astonishing that we have curatorial schools, but so little literature on the history of exhibition curating. Key texts are still missing. The writings of Pontus Hulten, Willem Sandberg, or Lucy Lippard—to take some absolutely indispensable examples—are out of print or difficult to find. (5)

―――――

The exhibition has this amazing advantage: that it's a ritual, it's extremely public. There isn't a prescribed time when people can visit it, or a prescribed length to their visit. They can visit it for a minute or for five hours or ten hours. (41)

―――――

Two summers ago, a taxi driver dropped me off [at the Serpentine] at 7 a.m. Because it was so early, he knew I couldn't be a visitor and asked me if I had some involvement in the galleries. When I said I was the director, he told me a story. He had been walking in Kensington Gardens one weekend with his wife and daughter, when the teenager ran into the Serpentine grounds. This man, who said he had never entered an art gallery because he didn't think it was for people like him, followed to fetch her back. All of a sudden he found himself in this incredible multicoloured structure—SelgasCano's pavilion—and realised he didn't actually dislike it. Ever since, his daughter has read only architecture books and all she wants to be is the next [Le] Corbusier. If we had charged even £1 entry, neither encounter would have happened. (70)

———

I often think of the example of the Belgian
artist—Jef Geys—who installed a painting
by [Pablo] Picasso inside a school.
Where better for a Picasso than
in a classroom?! (18)

———

I think it's really important that we take
barriers away, so that everybody can come,
particularly for kids whose parents don't think
it's a good idea to go to museums. (20)

———

The beauty of an exhibition is that it's a
nonlinear experience so you can return to a
painting. ... Pictures don't reveal themselves
instantly, it's important to be able to return. (64)

———

If we now look at what happened in the previous century, it's mainly through the artist's work that we can somehow experience these times. And I think in a way that will be the same for our time. Our time will be remembered through the artist. (61)

———

Look at the paintings of [Francisco José de] Goya: we barely remember the name of the King who commissioned them, but we will always remember Goya because art has very strong staying power, and it's a great thing to be at the service of art, to help artists, to enable art. (14)

———

The artists have to be in the center
of every museum. (33)

———

Exhibitions can and should go beyond simple
illustration or representation. They can
produce reality themselves. (73)

———

I think exhibitions are also laboratories.
They're a great place for artists to experiment
in public. It's not only about making the
work visible, of making the work public,
but it's also about experimenting with
how the work is shown. (61)

———

Curating is about making something,
but never on one's own. It's always a matter
of making something with someone else,
or for someone else, and always in
dialogue with artists. (2)

———

It is not good to have a premise and then
squeeze the artist into that vessel. (22)

———

Generally speaking, I have always tried
to avoid exhibitions that illustrate a curatorial
proposal, which I think is a very
limited concept. (68)

———

I think it's really interesting that there has been this strong period of separation through the modern age that moves towards specialization. That wasn't always the case. Look to Hildegard of Bingen, an abbess who was this major composer of the Middle Ages but also a writer, a poet, a healer, an early environmentalist. She's been a major inspiration for me—I like the Hildegards who don't think in terms of that separation. (53)

———

Our society is still very divided in lots of different silos and I think we need to build bridges; we don't need walls. (46)

———

I have always been interested in helping to build these bridges, to not only make art accessible, but to be what the Germans would call a *Wanderer Zwischen den Welten*, or a wanderer of worlds. To wander, to be upon, to stroll between worlds … that's an essential part of creativity. Because everything is connected; a bit like in string theory, which shows a surprising ability to connect things that do not appear to be connected on the surface. (57)

―――――

If you want to understand the forces which are active in art, I think one needs to also read science, one needs to read literature, one needs to read about music and architecture, all [of] these different fields. Just reading about art is not enough. (10)

Do It started out in the Café Sélect in Paris where Christian Boltanski, Bertrand Lavier, and I had a coffee in 1993. I was in my mid-20s. I had just started to curate exhibitions—my *Kitchen Show* was in 1991. (32)

We came up with the idea of an exhibition completely comprised of instruction manuals. We could give people little booklets of instructions, now printed in over a dozen languages. Artists write these manuals, and the artworks—which are performative— can be realized anywhere. It's an open-source exhibition. (11)

———

The project asks the visitor to act, not only to observe. (22)

———

On paper napkins, we started to write down names of artists whom we thought would most likely deliver fascinating instructions, even though they really hadn't used this modus operandi before. The list appeared infinite. (54)

———

Boltanski saw the instructions for installations as analogous to musical scores, which go through countless repetitions as they are interpreted and executed by others. (73)

———

Every realization of *Do It* is temporary:
an arrangement in space and an
activity in time. (73)

———

Someone recently asked me what has
been the most satisfactory experience in my
life as a curator. I responded that it was my
project *Do It*, which is a living archive of call
and response artworks that was started in
1993 with DIY art. It never stopped and
has now been in 165 cities. The greatest
fulfillment or achievement was when this
became part of the high school curriculum
in an education program in New York. (57)

———

Take Me (I'm Yours) is an exhibition we did for the Serpentine in the mid-'90s. It is now again on a tour. These exhibitions have a long life, and they evolve, so that kind of learning system—and they hopefully become smarter. They build up complexity over time. (16)

————

With *Take Me* (I'm Yours), we do not just bring the exhibition to a city and just throw it in: no, we listen. If the twentieth century has been a century of loudly proclaimed manifestoes, I think the twenty-first century needs to be very much a century of listening, both more listening, and an increased quality of listening. (20)

Utopia Station took shape as a conceptual as well as a physical structure, a place and a nonplace. It encompassed contributions from about sixty artists and architects, writers and performers, coordinated into a flexible plan by artists [Rirkrit] Tiravanija and the artist Liam Gillick. (73)[1]

———

I love this idea of creating platforms where something can happen, and so the curator is not the controller, but the releaser. (69)

———

1 *Utopia Station* was cocurated by Molly Nesbit, Rirkrit Tiravanija, and Hans Ulrich Obrist.

[Art is] not the recapitulation of something which existed, but there is an encounter with something we don't know yet, and that's unbelievably exciting. (57)

———

Over the years I've realized that younger generations of artists have a fluidity of practice now—from poetry to architecture to installations, all these different fields. So while as an exhibition maker I'm anchored in the visual arts world, I try to connect all the dots between different fields. (53)

———

I think curating involves working with many different disciplines but also many different generations of artists. (61)

———

Curating, in the sense of a distinct profession, is a fairly new thing. The activities it combines into one role, however, are still well expressed by the meaning [of] its Latin etymological root, curare: to take care of. (76)

———

The discussion of art's monetary value takes up a lot of space but I always felt that my role is to talk about everything but the money. (53)

———

Fundraising has become elemental to
the curatorial repertoire: to raise the budget
of one's exhibition is key in terms of securing
the continuation of programming autonomy.
(67)

I see myself as an enabler. (14)

I've always wanted to make salons for the
twenty-first century. (62)

I think that the attempt to find out
what art is[,] is really the permanent process.
If we had an answer to this question,
we'd probably stop. (62)

Artists and Conversations

I became a curator because I want to be helpful to artists—I think of my work as that of a catalyst and sparring partner. Central in what I do is the conversation with the artists. Everything grows out of that. (22)

―――――

A large part of my job is, of course, to look and look and look, but also to listen. We need to learn to listen to each other again. (53)

―――――

For me, the inspiration was David Sylvester.
I began to be interested in conversations with
artists because of an incredible book he did
with Francis Bacon. Whenever he met Francis
Bacon, he recorded the conversation. And little
by little they became this incredible book,
which, as a kid, I read again and again.
That's what pulled me into art. (64)

———

I never know if the word "interview" is
right. I call them "conversations," so it's
difficult to find a word for it. It's basically
an infinite conversation. (14)

———

Conversations are a way of archiving or preserving the past. (73)

―――――

The first encounter with an artist in person always remains a special moment for a curator. (59)

―――――

A conversation is a bit like how Wayne Shorter describes jazz: jumping into the unknown. But free-form also requires a lot of preparation, which is kind of a paradox. (45)

―――――

During an artist conversation, I can't look into my computer or into my BlackBerry. Often I go into the conversation with a pile of paper and then pull a question from my notes. I never ask questions in a given order, but I have a sort of cluster on a sheet of paper. (39)

———

I have a large stack of cards where there are hundreds of different questions. Very often it is up to chance how these cards are sequenced and how questions are raised. In this sense, I am extremely prepared, but I also try to leave the interview open to improvisation. (71)

———

I'm always working with artists, architects, or scientists—either on a show or on a conference or a book, and very often the conversation is not only parallel to working on a project, but new projects even grow out of the conversations. So, one can actually call them "production of reality" conversations. (63)

―――――――

Conversations are where I can forget about time, or even liberate time. (50)

―――――――

My approach to interviews, particularly
as they relate to fields other than my own, is
probably motivated by the desire to remain a
student eager to learn. Every time I go to see
a scientist or an architect I try to read everything they have written, as if I were
preparing for a seminar. (39)

When I'm preparing for a conversation,
I like to study the multiple histories of
a person, and I end up with hundreds of
pages of script with which to go into the
conversation and ask questions. But it
always ends up being very much about
order and disorder. (81)

Talking to people is very fascinating for me, but so is the process that gets you there, which has a lot to do with reading and scripting. (81)

———

I don't really have a master plan. I somehow go from one thing to the next, driven by curiosity. Curiosity is one of my engines. (14)

———

A conversation is a synchronous communication in space and involves gestures, visual signals, and a variety of voices; whereas an exchange lacks the embodied presence of speech. Very often it falls between these two extremes. And this obviously leads to the big problem of silences, because there are things that cannot be transcribed. (71)

———

Christian Boltanski and Paul-Armand Gette, who were professors of Fine Art, told me about a genius artist in their class called Koo Jeong-A and they introduced us. I saw the works she was in the process of making on the inaccessible or the invisible. She used everyday objects—sugarcubes, stamps—and explored the contact we have with such objects. She created little houses, architectures, cities with bits of sugar and planks of wood; she also made installations out of chewing gum. Very soon, we were living together. It was the most important meeting of my life. (3)

Koo started off from generic objects, sugarcubes or magnets, everyday things, and constructed the most fantastical, visionary, and in some ways utopian architectures. Magnetism dictates the form, the relief, the construction. It is very mathematical, and she does very complex calculations for her pieces. (3)

———

It's kind of overwhelming when suddenly the person takes things somewhere that you didn't expect. (81)

———

Interviews happen in strange situations. For example, with Anri Sala, we travel a lot. ... Whenever we have a minute we record things, and make what you might describe as "interviews on the move." It is a very physical activity and a collective project. (50)

———

Whenever I do exhibitions and books, they are the outcomes of such conversations— conversations with artists, conversations with architects, scientists, all kinds of practitioners. So, one can basically say that the conversations are not conversations for conversation's sake, but are always working conversations. (63)

———

I've curated the Dakar Biennale. I've curated
different biennials in Guangzhou, Shanghai,
and Seoul. I've curated shows in Brazil, and in
Mexico, and many other places in Latin
America. Each time I go into a new context,
I come out a different person. (2)

———

Even once I started to curate bigger biennales
and bigger art shows I always returned to
smaller exhibition formats so as not to lose
that intimacy. I think there is a very different
form of conversation going on, and also artists
would do other kinds of works than they
would do in a monumental space. (27)

———

I don't think that the curator has brilliant
ideas in which the artists then should fit.
Instead, it always starts with a conversation,
where I ask the artists what their unrealized
projects are, and then the task is to find means
to realize these projects in a pragmatic way.
At our first meeting, Boetti said to me that
if I succeed in this task, then I would
be a curator. (76)

———

A successful collaboration is complementary.
(52)

———

Archiving, Collecting,
and Unrealized Projects

Like many children, I collected the Panini pictures of football players, which you glue into an album. My grandfather was a great stamp collector, so he encouraged me to collect stamps at some point. There were coins when I was very small. At a certain moment, I was collecting all kinds of T-shirts. (25)

———

It was very attractive—magnetically attractive—to me, seeing these paintings and artworks reproduced, so I also started to buy up postcards of artworks. (72)

———

I built up a huge archive of thousands
and thousands of [postcards], like my own
imaginary museum: a section on Picasso,
a section on [Paul] Cézanne, a section on
[Claude] Monet, a section on Bacon,
and so on. (72)

―――――

Those 5,000 postcards were my first archive.
With them, I started to curate my own
exhibitions. Then the postcards led to my own
portable museum—the Nano Museum. In the
early 1990s, I invited artists to make these
little, framed, two-by-three-inch works, and
I carried them wherever I went. (25)

―――――

The museum went with me wherever I went.
I would show it to all [of] my friends and also
to strangers, wherever I would be. (61)

―――――

I made my studio visit with Fischli/Weiss
in '87 and ever since I've had conversations
with artists, but unfortunately, the first
conversations were not recorded, so they're
lost. It's only at the beginning of the '90s that
I started to realize that I had gaps in my
memory and I wanted to go back to certain
conversations. I felt it's a pity not to have
a recording, so I started to make audio
recordings of my conversations. (61)

―――――

Various happenstances led me to do videos. One involved Jonas Mekas, with whom I've worked a lot, and who said, "You should just film them, like I do, you just have a little camera on the table, and one day you will be very happy to have it." So, I'm deeply grateful to Jonas, because maybe a third of my conversations have also been filmed.

(45)

———

Then I went to Chicago to see Studs Terkel, he's one of the greatest oral historians of the twentieth century, and he said, "It needs to be a bit shaky and improvised because if you are too good at technology, and you have this really posh equipment, it's intimidating to people." So I never have a tripod, I often put the camera or the phone into a coffee cup, or on a book, and then at some point it collapses and falls on the floor. (45)

———

Initially it was all with these mini-DV cassettes. The last six or seven years have obviously been iPhone recordings. Finally, 2020 was all Zoom videos. (49)

———

[The year 2021], strangely, has actually been the most productive year because I probably recorded 500 or 600 conversations. Because of COVID-19, I did Zoom conversations every day. (45)

———

I do not spend much time archiving, although I do have a nighttime collaborator, Max Shackleton, who works for me through to 6 a.m. and does most of the archiving of my digital interviews. (21)

———

I am convinced that if you look back
too much and become your own archivist,
you can create a situation where you
block the future. (21)

———

I hope my work is a utility. (61)

———

There are other archives, also: the archives
of my notes, the archives of my doodles.
The photographs I take; I've started to
make portraits of all of the artists, so I
have an archive of thousands and
thousands of portraits. (72)

———

Writing is a production of reality. (52)

———

Archives have long ceased to be the sole concern of museums and administrations—in the digital age each of us has archives to store photos, emails, text messages, and films. (75)

———

Memory is very radical right now. My obsessive interviewing with very old practitioners, those who are almost 100 years old, clearly has to do with Eric Hobsbawm's protest against forgetting. In the world in which we are living—one constantly defined by newness—nobody talks about age. (61)

———

Memory is not a simple record of events but a dynamic process that always transforms what it dredges up from its depths, and the conversation has become my way to instigate such a process. (73)

———

You can never reconstitute an exhibition, you can only try to archive a combination of all its different aspects. (12)

———

How do you document the smell of an exhibition, how do you document the sound of an exhibition? (12)

———

Some of my exhibitions can be restaged in fifty or a hundred years, without me, without the artist, just by following the discourse. I want them to be brought back to life constantly. They evolve, grow, and breathe. (21)

———

It was Rosemarie Trockel, the German artist, who always said how important it would be, that there would be a trace not only of artists I meet that are living and working now. She said I should really go and see very senior artists. She encouraged me to go and see centenarians. (61)

———

Most of curatorial history is oral history;
it's very much a story that can only be told
because it's not yet been written. (73)

————

The motor, the engine, is curiosity.
Curating is connected to curiosity. (43)

————

I think that my interviews project is so
far 4,000 hours—and it is because I want
to share my conversations with artists
with other people. (43)

————

Conversations are obviously archival, but they are also a form of creating fertile soil for future projects. For this reason, I began to ask everyone I interviewed a very future-oriented question: what is your unrealized project, your dream? (73)

———

My meeting with Alighiero Boetti changed my life in a day. One of the first things he advised me to do was always to ask about artists' unrealized projects in my conversations with them. I have done it ever since. (76)

The other day, somebody asked me
what my most important archive is, and
I've started to think it's actually the thousands
of answers I hear, in my conversations,
about unrealized projects. (25)

———

Since 1990, I have been gathering
information on thousands of unrealized
artists' projects—roads not taken—as a
kind of a "reservoir of ideas." There are the
forgotten projects, the directly or indirectly
censored projects, the partially realized
projects, the misunderstood projects, the
oppressed projects, the lost projects, the
unrealizable projects: all between
the nonreal and the probable. (74)

———

I think we all have projects which we haven't dared to do or haven't yet dared to do. (61)

―――――

With architects, we always know about their unrealized projects. But with artists, philosophers, and writers, you often never find out about their dreams or their unrealized projects. (82)

―――――

My questions are always about what we could do together, what one could build, what is unbuilt. (25)

―――――

There are many amazing unrealized projects out there: forgotten projects, misunderstood projects, lost projects, desk-drawer projects, poetic-utopian dream projects, unrealizable projects, partially realized projects, censored projects, and so on. (38)

———

I'm not only always asking artists about their unrealized projects, but I also have a whole roster of unrealized projects that I want to do. (36)

———

I would like to dedicate an enduring institution to these unresearched products of creativity. Therefore, my big project is a palace of unrealized projects. (75)

———

Édouard Glissant and
Mondialité

I have a ritual of reading Édouard Glissant's books for fifteen minutes every morning. His poems, novels, plays, and theoretical essays are a toolbox I use every day. (17)

———

Édouard Glissant, who was born Martinique in 1928 and died in Paris on 3 February 2011, was one of the most important writers and philosophers of our time. He called attention to means of global exchange that do not homogenise culture but produce a difference from which new things can emerge. (17)

———

What is so radical about Glissant's thinking
is not only its prescience, but also the breadth
of its relevance and possible application today.
(17)

———

I was first introduced to Glissant's
thinking through Alighiero Boetti, whom
I met right after turning eighteen in 1986.
Throughout the second half of the 1990s
I got to know Glissant in the company of
our mutual friend agnès b. Our friendship
started in Parisian cafés, and these meetings
quickly became rituals. (56)

———

"Archipelic thought," which endeavours to do justice to the world's diversity, forms an antithesis to continental thought, which makes a claim to absoluteness and tries to force its singular worldview on others. (73)

―――

For Glissant, what is so significant about the Antillean archipelagos is the fact that they are an island group that has no centre but consists of a string of different islands and cultures.

(17)

―――

Against the homogenizing forces of globalization Glissant coined the term *mondialité* ("globality"), which refers to forms of world-wide exchange that recognize and preserve diversity and creolization. (73)

―――

Glissant's idea of mondialité invites us instead to negotiate everyday contemporaneity by beginning, not from the homogenizing, inward-looking perspective of competing continents, but from the open, relational perspective offered by thinking of nations as strung together like archipelagos. (2)

He is really the model for all [of] my exhibitions, such as Do It or Cities on the Move. He says that today, we can actually project ourselves in the global and local at the same time—"glocal" in a way. We have been seeking an effect between the global and the local, where every location has its own dimension and vision. (30)

Glissant always said that it's important
to be rooted and we need to think about
the local, but this idea of being local or rooted
is only important as long as it does not lead
to the exclusion of other people's roots. Then
it becomes very dangerous—it leads to
nationalism, lack of tolerance, all [of]
these things we observed during
the COVID crisis. (48)

So we should use technology for a global dialogue, not for isolation. It's a conundrum, and Glissant describes it very beautifully: how can we negotiate these two things and not fall into the trap of new nationalisms and new regionalisms that reject globalization? How can we embrace the potential of this global dialogue in a way that doesn't alienate differences? (14)

In the '80s, the Western Hemisphere concentrated itself only on a few art centers. Everything was focused on these centers. But now we have multiple centers. Every center is surrounded by many other centers. The quest for the absolute center seems redundant. (60)

———

There is a lot of pressure on curators to do shows not only in one place, but to send them around the world by simply packing them into boxes in one city and unpacking them in the next—this is a homogenizing sort of globalization. (74)

———

The globalization we find ourselves in today is certainly not the first historical phase of cultural interaction and transactions in the world, but the third or fourth. Considering the events of recent times, however, we are undoubtedly in one of globalization's most extreme and violent phases. (17)

———

Homogenized globalization leads to extinction, leads to a disappearance of species, but also disappearance of cultural phenomena. We are losing many languages which are disappearing at a faster speed than ever before. (7)

———

[Glissant] criticized the classical utopias, such as Plato's *Republic* and Thomas More's *Utopia*, for being conceived as static systems. He designed a new, alternative form of utopia consisting of a continuous dialogue. (17)

———

The most important thing [Glissant] told me is that he imagined this island, or utopia, to be a quivering place, which transcends established systems of thought, and is looking for the utopian point where all the world's cultures and imaginations can meet and hear one another. For me, it has a lot to do with listening. (45)

———

I do have an unrealized dream for a trip. Glissant wanted to build a museum in Martinique, which he told me would help us to look from a utopian point at all the world's cultures. We had been planning to go together by boat, because he would always travel by boat to Martinique, and that trip remained unrealized when he passed away. (48)

———

The core of my conversation project is to learn to listen. This idea that we can maybe create the archive where all the world's cultures and all the world's imaginations can meet and hear one another. (45)

———

On Sleep and Time

It's important that we liberate time because otherwise we can no longer be playful. Otherwise we just somehow are locked in our own system of being busy. (7)

———

It is striking to see how many artists used the iconography of the bed in their artworks. It is probably one of the most powerful metaphors for the human condition. Life usually starts in beds and very often ends there. There are the big topics of art such as death, life, love, or fear, and in a way, these topics are all very much related to sleep and the bed. (8)

———

There is an interesting book by Jonathan Crary called 24/7 in which he cautions against our permanent availability. With every new device or medium, you become more available and accessible and [see] how time is being modernized and standardized. This ties in with what philosopher Édouard Glissant had to say about *mondialité* and how globalization forces us to redefine time and space. It is extremely important to delink and break free from this 24/7 circle and that usually happens at night when we sleep. (8)

When I was younger, I went against
my internal clock almost daily. It produced
some interesting ideas but it's not a
sustainable lifestyle. (8)

———

I grew up in Switzerland. I started to relent-
lessly work and seldom sleep. … It maybe has
to do with rebellion, against the imposed
homogenized time frame in which we are
living, or in which we are all supposed to
live—24 hours, with eight hours sleep, eight
hours work, eight hours leisure. I always
felt that was an imposition. (24)

———

[Leonardo da] Vinci had this rhythm where he would only sleep for 15 minutes every three hours. As an experiment, I did this for almost a year. It's how I wrote my first books. Now I sleep much more because it wasn't fully sustainable. (7)

———

Changing your structure is important because you make different experiences and can learn from them. (8)

———

The moment you fall asleep, you give up every bit of conscious control over your body and mind. There is the saying that every day is a new life and hence you die every single night and are reborn every morning. (8)

———

I was very fascinated by the productivity and the sheer output of [Honoré de] Balzac. I was just embarking on my first book project and it took me forever. I kept thinking about how I could increase my output and reach a more dynamic form of productivity. When I found out that Balzac's productivity was fueled by an immense amount of coffee—up to 52 cups a day—I thought that his method was worth exploring and so I tried it out for a year. ... I probably drank between 30 and 40 cups a day but often just small espressos. There were, however, days when I did reach the Balzacian threshold. (8)

———

Drinking a lot of coffee, lots and lots of it, became my first morning ritual. I regularly ordered between 10 and 20 espressos in the café. Of course, from a health point of view, that was not sustainable, and I had to come up with something else. (75)

———

Each of us has within us a clock which tells us how we need to live our lives, the routine we need to follow. (6)

———

I realized that for a long time I had tried to force myself into some weird, absurd sleeping rhythm, and I needed to identify my own. And my own rhythm is that I sleep every night from midnight to 5:45 a.m. (24)

―――――

Once I understood the importance of my internal clock, I started to organize my entire life accordingly. (8)

―――――

I can't sleep unless I read something in bed. It's not only a place I go to sleep but also to read and unwind. So I always take a lot of books with me when I am traveling to make myself at home. (8)

———

Today we live in a situation where we have a lot of communication with devices but without community. These devices can be quite isolating. So I've always had an inclination to introduce rituals to my life. For example, I buy a book every day. Another ritual is the night train. (7)

Every morning when I wake up I go through lots of rituals: reading Édouard Glissant, and jogging, and writing in a notebook—but one main ritual without which a day really never starts is making a cyber introduction by email. I think about people I could bring together and then send emails saying, "I feel it's urgent that you meet," and then these people meet and sometimes something happens. (48)

——

I think the idea of the ritual is interesting because, of course, it involves a certain repetition, a certain stability, even if they're different each time. (7)

——

Art and the Environment

I think, if we want to address the big question or challenges of the twenty-first century—if it's extinction, ecology, inequality, or the future of technology—it's very important that we go beyond the fear of pooling knowledge and move beyond these silos of knowledge to bring the different disciplines together. (7)

———

We can use technology for fostering attention to the natural world. We need to look at how tech can create a spiritual connection with nature to make sure we are communicating with the environment rather than continue this colonial separation from nature, which is destroying the environment. It is about expanding the possibilities of how art can act as an intermediate between culture, technology, and society, and how art can liberate us from becoming stuck in a quantified world, which is very dangerous. (35)

The notions of ecology and collaboration through "long-duration programming" are very much embedded within my project "do it," which began in Paris in 1993 as a set of instructions that were distributed as a book, inviting artists and others to interpret the ideas and build whatever they saw within. In devising this new format for a show, I was concerned with how exhibitions could be rendered more flexible and open-ended; an "art for all" expansion into other circuits, which encourages greater levels of participation and interaction on the part of the audience. The result is a show that is always locally produced with reusable materials so that no resources are wasted. (19)

Resistance is an expression of hope in the future. I always think of Jean-François Lyotard, who wanted to put together a group exhibition called *Resistances*. He said that the problem with exhibitions is that they take place and then come apart. He considered it urgent to create an exhibition that would continue long after doors to the exhibition space were closed. The success of the exhibition would instead be measured by the connections established between people, who would then collaborate. (18)

———

It is important to address the many ways in which our futures could unfold. Declaring ourselves in a state of inevitabilities is an attempt to shirk responsibility. (77)

———

I think the impulse of archiving and of collecting is maybe also believing that there is a future, believing that we are not going to be an extinct species. (25)

———

More and more artists are building gardens and farms. So artwork becomes a living organism but in an analog sense. (47)

———

Ecology has been at the very heart of the LUMA Foundation since its formation by Maja Hoffmann. Around 2007, Maja invited me to participate in a meeting of the group in Zurich with the artists Liam Gillick and Philippe Parreno and the curators Tom Eccles and Beatrix Ruf. She had a vision of creating a new arts centre [that]… would have a sort of ecologist poetic and a new sensibility with regard to the Earth and the planet. And for this project she wanted to surround herself with artists and curators from the start. (3)

———

When you build a center for the art of the future, you don't know what the art or the exhibition or even the urgent issues of the future might be. So for this reason an archipelago aiming to do justice to the diversity of the world, an archipelago that is an antithesis of continental European thought, has more chance of capturing this than a continental structure that, in its absolute form, tries to impose a point of view on the world. (3)

———

LUMA is not just about exhibitions,
it [is] a structure that persists, that
continues, that doesn't stop. (3)

———

I think that storytelling can create empathy.
I think the potential in art lies in how artists
always change what we expect from them.
We should always be open to artists coming
up with new ways of dealing with emergen-
cies. Hope is important, that's why
we need new stories. (23)

———

I believe we've reached a time when every organization, whether it's a political party, a government, a corporation, or a brand, should include artists in their decision-making processes as artists John Latham and Barbara Steveni suggested through their artist placement group. (4)

———

We live in a time where we can only tackle the big issues and changes of the twenty-first century if we go beyond our fear of pooling knowledge and collaborating across all sectors. The climate crisis requires us to create new alliances. (15)

———

I think there is a distinction to be made between the global and the planetary. The global is very much centred on the human being. If we think in terms of global, it touches upon what humans have done to each other, but also to the planet, to nature. So it is a history that is very centred on the human being. It is essentially during the last five centuries or so that we have had this more or less irreversible impact on our planet. The planetary, on the other hand, is much longer, it amounts to two billion years, the age of the Earth. Consequently its scale is geological and biological. (3)

———

Instead of adopting escape strategies from the earth, we need to adopt "back to earth" strategies. What we are seeing now, is a general rehearsal leading us to the main spectacle, which is climate change. Judy Chicago wrote a manifesto where she said we need an art of substance, an art of meaning and substance. It's not about going back—it's about changing. (44)

In this age where information is abundant but memory often falls short, I think it's important to acknowledge the artists who have contributed to the discourse on the climate emergency since the start of the movement. In my field, Gustav Metzger springs to mind, who has been at the forefront of this struggle since the 60s/70s really. Then there's Agnes Denes, whose seminal 1969 manifesto resonates powerfully today. And the Harrisons who contributed a manifesto that criminalized plastic for our ongoing Back to Earth program at Serpentine. (4)

It's important to have slower travel. ... We need a movement to reintroduce night trains, and to introduce them in places they have not existed. One further characteristic of slower travel is to stay for lengthier periods of time if long distance trips are necessary, a longer engagement with the condition of a specific place. (48)

———

Images are powerful. If images rule dreams, and dreams rule actions, artists have a particular responsibility at this critical juncture of human civilization. We need to use all the agency we have to nurture a new planetary visualization of the embeddedness and codependency of our species with all others—art against extinction.

(19)

———

As Gerhard Richter told me, art is the highest form of hope. (15)

Technology and the
Future of Art

Art provides new ways of thinking about the present and thinking about the future. Never has it been more important to share that knowledge. (18)

———

Technology often creates separation. Social media creates filters. With art we can hopefully break that filter bubble, and be an intermediator between culture, art, science, technology. It's about togetherness. (35)

———

A crucial question of the twenty-first century is how to foster collective action in the age of the internet. (12)

———

Now more than ever, the dream is to be able to possess the agency to create new worlds, not just inherit and live within existing ones. (55)

———

We must acknowledge and encourage difference. (17)

———

If there was ever a time that the world needed artists, it is now. We need their radical ideas, visions, and perspectives in society. (31)

———

The ritual of the exhibition is more
important than ever before. Millions of
people visit exhibitions every day, and
I think it's important that it's not
an abstract entity. (34)

———

In a field that has very much to do with the
experiential, it is very important that you go
through the experience of actually visiting an
exhibition, and in this sense the exhibition
is very haptic and physical. ... The same is
true for the book, which hasn't disappeared
at all in the digital age. (9)

———

The reason why so many visitors all over
the world want to engage with this ritual
of the exhibition has a lot to do with the fact
that it's an experience that you can't have at
home in front of your computer. (34)

———

Often with virtual reality, the goggle in an
exhibition isolates you from all the other
people. This is why I think AR [augmented
reality] and mixed reality have a bigger
potential. (42)

———

The internet is changing the structure of our brains and the structure of our planet in extraordinary ways, so quickly that we haven't yet developed a proper vocabulary for it. (11)

———

It's important that we not just explain and didactically show, but also give visitors a chance for experience. The question is not should we use AI or not use AI, but how can we use AI as a potential while ethically sourcing data without appropriating the entire life of someone not being credited or compensated in any way. We need artists in this discussion. Artists have really important things to contribute to the whole debate, so we need to put artists in the places where actual decisions are made. (47)

———

Our task now should be to collectively think about how we can use these technologies to turn them into the opposite—that is, how we can use these technologies to create togetherness and not separation, a common future and not isolation. (46)

———

Technological progress has accelerated to the point that the future is happening to us far faster than we could ever have anticipated. This new world is what we call "extreme present," a time in which it feels impossible to maintain pace with the present, never mind to chart the future. (11)

The artists of our time, of course, are now working with the Internet, digital images, and artificial intelligence. Their works and thoughts again are an early alarm system for the developments ahead of us. (26)

———

We must trust in artists to discover new ways of thinking about the present and the future. (18)

———

Artists have antennae that allow them [to] anticipate things. (53)

———

Artists can not only show us how to positively use these technologies, but also show us the dark corridors of technology, the dangers, which is equally important. ... Artists can make the invisible visible. (35)

I think all art forms can be a portal which opens worlds. If you think about artists as world-makers, you can see artworks opening doors to these worlds we had not known could exist before. At this moment, we realize it's not about illustrating previously established findings. (57)

If we invent the future, it's very often
with fragments from the past. (61)

———

Whenever I make studio visits now, many
artists—not only tech artists but others who
work in more traditional mediums—have a
dream to make a video game. (47)

———

Video games represent a form of worldbuilding—something art has been doing
forever. The creation of games offers a unique
opportunity for world-building: rules can
be set up, surroundings, systems, and
dynamics can be built and altered,
new realms can emerge. (55)

———

Traditionally, video games were created
by a small and insular group of people
coming from the world of engineering and
producing games with a very limited perspective. This is now changing rapidly, with many
more people having access to the tools
for making games. (78)

———

Gaming is becoming to our time what movies
were to the twentieth century and what novels
were to the nineteenth century. (55)

———

There are many parts of our lives which are based on bonuses and rewards. Incentive systems that we are not aware of shape our desires. Sometimes we start playing games we don't even want to play. So, we play the game, but the game plays us. We need to be wary of that. (29)

———

It is important to make knowledge more accessible, in part by linking it to play. Video games are a means of communication in this century and can create new cohesion. (15)

———

We can heighten awareness of the ever-increasing proliferation of technology in our everyday lives, whilst looking to artists for guidance in how we might navigate this shifting terrain. (26)

At this moment in time, it is more urgent than ever that we platform artists so that they have a seat at the table as powerful new technologies play increasingly important roles in shaping the future of society. (26)

Data can be transformed into art when artists liberate the poetic and intercultural dimension of data. (51)

The idea of an artwork never being the same twice is quite new, and it's enabled by artists that operate with technology. These artworks are not stable: they are unstable. Our archives are not stable. (46)

———

I am interested in developing archives for exhibitions to be played and replayed. (21)

———

I am particularly struck by the fact that there's a whole new form of poetry in the digital age. (2)

———

[Believing in art] in part is about how we decide to liberate society from short-termism—this idea that we live in a 24/7 society in which more and more things are based on short-term deadlines. In order to address the urgent topics of our time, to transcend that short-termism, I think that leads us directly to art. It's hard for anything to last, and nothing does that better than art. (53)

———

Gerhard Richter once told me that art is the highest form of hope. In a secular society, art often takes on the function that religion has had in previous times. And I've always felt very strongly that art and artists give me hope. (53)

———

SOURCES

Quotes have been lightly edited by the author

1. Segalov, Michael. "Sunday with Hans Ulrich-Obrist: 'I Go to London Zoo—Mostly for the Architecture.'" *Guardian*, January 5, 2020. https://www.theguardian.com/lifeand style/2020/jan/05/sunday-with-hans-ulrich-obrist-i-go -to-london-zoo-mostly-for-the-architecture.

2. Smith, Terry. "Curating as Medium." Interview of Hans Ulrich Obrist by Terry Smith. In *Talking Contemporary Curat-ing*, edited by Terry Smith, 114–38. New York: Independent Curators International, November 24, 2015.

3. Obrist, Hans Ulrich. *Une vie in progress*. Paris: Seuil, April 7, 2023. English translation unpublished.

4. Obrist, Hans Ulrich. "A Trembling Utopia: Hans Ulrich Obrist in Conversation with Nikolaj Schultz." Office, May 31, 2024. https://officemagazine.net/trembling -utopia-hans-ulrich-obrist-conversation-nikolaj-schultz.

5. Obrist, Hans Ulrich. Text for speech at Symposium at the Brooklyn Museum in conjunction with E-Flux, November 11–21, 2016.

6. Obrist, Hans Ulrich. Unpublished proposal for text *Liberate Time*, 2016.

7. Funk, Mia. "Hans-Ulrich Obrist Interviewed by Mia Funk." *Creative Process*, 2020. https://www.creativeprocess.info /art/hans-ulrich-obrist-mia-funk-slnsa.

8. Obrist, Hans Ulrich. "Sleep Interview." Unpublished.

9. Herman, Laura. "TLmag 25 Extended: Alpine Creatives." *TL mag*, July 8, 2016. https://tlmagazine.com/hans-ulrich -obrist/.

10. King, Emily. "The Interview: Hans Ulrich Obrist." *Happy Reader*, 2016.

11. "Living in the Extreme Present—*Real Review* Interviews Hans-Ulrich Obrist." *Real Review*, November 22, 2016.

12. Slager, Henk. "Conversation on Experimentality with Henk Slager." *Colophon*, 2016.

13. Lointier, Mylène Ferrand. "Hans Ulrich Obrist, Reflections on the Exhibition Reset Modernity! at ZKM." *Seismopolite*, August 10, 2016.

14. Martin Nova interviews Hans Ulrich Obrist on his book *Conversations in Columbia*. Unpublished, 2016.

15. "The Right Collisions between Art and Fashion: A Conversation between Hans-Ulrich Obrist and Gianluigi Ricuperati." Unpublished.

16. Burns, Charlotte. "The Art World: In Other Words, Art Can Change the World, with Hans Ulrich Obrist." *Art World: What If …?!*, August 17, 2017. https://inotherwords .libsyn.com/episode-13-art-can-change-the-world-with -hans-ulrich-obrist.

17. Obrist, Hans Ulrich. *Mondialité* text. Unpublished, 2017.

18. Obrist, Hans Ulrich. Draft for speech at SVA Curatorial Practice Summit. Unpublished, 2017. https://www.macp .sva.edu/2017-summita3n.

19. Obrist, Hans Ulrich. "Art against Extinction." *NOĒMA*, April 13, 2021.

20. Obrist, Hans Ulrich. Lecture on Art and Technology at the Saas-Fee Institute, Switzerland, 2018.

21. Alessandrini, Michela. "The Polyphonic Archive, Hans Ulrich Obrist." In *Curatorial Archives in Curatorial Practices*, edited by Michela Alessandrini, 107–12. Istanbul: Salt, 2018. https://saltonline.org/media/files/ollected_in _curatorial_practices__scrd-2.pdf.

22. Comte, Claudia. Interview with Hans Ulrich Obrist. Unpublished, December 2018.

23. Birnbaum, Astrid. "The Junction Maker." *Nuda*, July 9, 2024. https://nudapaper.com/the-junction-maker/.

24. Obrist, Hans Ulrich. "Brutally Early Club Interview." Unpublished, February 2018.

25. Emina, Seb. "Hans Ulrich Obrist—Collecting, Archiving & Curating." *Cereal* 16 (Autumn–Winter 2018): 126–28.

26. Obrist, Hans Ulrich. "The Future Flies in Under the Radar." Unpublished, 2024.

27. Lasch, Cassandra Edlefsen. "Hans Ulrich Obrist in Conversation with Cassandra Edlefsen Lasch." Recorded interview

screened with Homecomings Symposium, October 10, 2014.

28. "Hans Ulrich Obrist: 'I Believe in Generosity as a Medium.'" *Talks*. https://the-talks.com/interview/hans-ulrich-obrist/.

29. Obrist, Hans Ulrich. Interview with Chiara Parisi. *Connaissance des Artes*, June 12, 2023. English translation unpublished.

30. Guo, Sophie X. "2019 Shanghai Urban Space Art Season: On the Urgency of Public Art." *SUSAS*, 2019. English translation unpublished. https://www.sohu.com/a/437921117_725681.

31. Obrist, Hans Ulrich. "It's Urgent." Speech at the Heartland Festival, Kværndrup, Denmark, 2019.

32. Presa, Elizabeth. "Hans Ulrich Obrist on *Do It*." Interview for *Do It: The Compendium* in collaboration with Independent Curators International, 2019.

33. Imhof, Dora, and Christina Bechtler. Interview for publication "Museum of the Future." *JRP*, January 2015.

34. Obrist, Hans Ulrich. Exhibition text for *15 Rooms*. Shanghai, 2014. https://waysofcurating.withgoogle.com/exhibition/rooms-exhibitions-shanghai.

35. Banks, Nargess. "Serpentine Artistic Director Hans Ulrich Obrist on the Critical Role of Cultural Spaces in the AI Age." *Forbes*, June 27, 2024. https://www.forbes.com

/sites/nargessbanks/2024/06/27/interview-hans-ulrich
-obrist/.

36. Wallace, Brett. "A Conversation with Hans Ulrich Obrist."
    Conversation Project NYC, January 23, 2020. http://www
    .conversationprojectnyc.com/interviews/2020/5/14
    /a-conversation-with-hans-ulrich-obrist.

37. Obrist, Hans Ulrich. "A History of the Unrealised /
    Part 1." *Flash Art*, May 2020. https://flash---art
    .com/2020/05/a-history-of-the-unrealised-part-i/.

38. Obrist, Hans Ulrich. "Biennial Manifesto." *Flash Art*,
    November 14, 2016. https://flash---art.com/article
    /biennial-manifesto/.

39. Ursprung, Philip. "Curiosity Is the Motor of the Entire
    Interview Project. Hans Ulrich Obrist in Conversation with
    Philip Ursprung." *Art Bulletin* 94, no. 1 (March 2012):
    42–49.

40. Szántó, András. "Ecology & Slow Programming." In *The
    Future of the Museum: 28 Dialogues*, 191–201. Berlin: Hatje
    Cantz, 2021.

41. Hans Ulrich Obrist interviewed by John Brockman for the
    Edge Foundation, April 7, 2014.

42. Iwata, Tomoya. "The Future of Curationship with Technol-
    ogy." Catalog for *Alter-Narratives* at the Department of Arts
    Studies and Curatorial Practices, Graduate School of Global
    Arts, Tokyo University of the Arts, 2020. https://ga.geidai
    .ac.jp/en/portfolio/hans-ulrich-obrist/.

43. Elkann, Alain. "Hans Ulrich Obrist." *Alain Elkann Interviews*, April 5, 2020. https://www.alainelkanninterviews.com/hans-ulrich-obrist/.

44. Lauf, Cornelia, and Stefano Boeri. "We Must Become Idealists to Confront This World: Hans Ulrich Obrist in Conversation with Stefano Boeri." *Lampoon Magazine*, November 5, 2020.

45. Zahm, Olivier. "Hans Ulrich Obrist." *Purple* 35 (Spring–Summer 2021). https://purple.fr/magazine/the-island-issue-35/hans-ulrich-obrist/.

46. "Our Society Is Still Very Divided in Lots of Different Silos and I Think We Need to Build Bridges, We Don't Need Walls." *Many of Them* 8 (June–July July 2021): 44–53.

47. Battaglia, Andy. "Curator Hans Ulrich Obrist on a Dynamic 'Year of AI' at Serpentine in London." *Artnews*, August 20, 2024. https://www.artnews.com/art-news/news/curator-hans-ulrich-obrist-artificial-intelligence-serpentine-galleries-london-1234714858/.

48. Rosenberg, Karen. "The Artful Travel Interview: Hans Ulrich Obrist." *Artful Jaunts*, July 8, 2021. https://www.artfuljaunts.com/magazine/the-artful-travel-interview-hans-ulrich-obrist.

49. Ascari, Alessio. "Office Goals." *Kaleidoscope* 38 (Spring–Summer 2021).

50. Haq, Nav. "A Conversation with Hans Ulrich Obrist."

Bidoun, Fall 2006. https://www.bidoun.org/articles /hans-ulrich-obrist.

51. Odukoya, Olu. "Kunst Talk: Hans Ulrich Obrist. Olu Odukoya in Conversation with Hans Ulrich Obrist." *Modern Matter*, 2021. https://amodernmatter.com/article /kunst-talk-hans-ulrich-obrist/.

52. Obrist, Hans Ulrich. *Conversations in Mexico*. Mexico City: Fundacíon Alumnos47, 2016.

53. Sims, Josh. "Interview: Hans Ulrich Obrist." *A Collected Man*, June 2022. https://www.acollectedman.com/blogs /journal/interview-hans-ulrich-obrist.

54. Obrist, Hans Ulrich. "Do It." In … *dontstopdontstopdontstop-dontstop*, edited by April Elizabeth Lamm, 92–98. London: Sternberg, 2006.

55. Lok, Kate. "Culture in Simulation: Hans Ulrich Obrist on the Relevance of Gaming, and the Art of Today." *Artazine*, October 20, 2022. https://www.artazine.com/features /hans-ulrich-obrist-worldbuilding-gaming-art-julia -stoschek-collection.

56. Obrist, Hans Ulrich. "The Archipelago Conversations, an Excerpt—Interview with Edouard Glissant." *European Review of Books* 2 (December 19, 2022). https:// europeanreviewofbooks.com/the-archipelago -conversations-an-excerpt/.

57. Röder, Seda, and Hans Ulrich Obrist. "Portals to New

Worlds." In *Creativity Matters: Inspiring Insights from Real Life for Real People*, edited by Maryam Ghaddar, 18–23. Salzburg: Sonophilia Foundation, 2020.

58. "TEDxMarrakesh—Hans Ulrich Obrist—The Art of Curating." TEDx Talks. October 10, 2011. Video, 19:53. https://www.youtube.com/watch?v=gyIVCqf23cA.

59. Obrist, Hans Ulrich. "First Encounter with Mark Manders." In … dontstopdontstopdontstopdontstop, edited by April Elizabeth Lamm, 103–4. London: Sternberg, 2006.

60. Obrist, Hans Ulrich. "Coffee in the Kitchen." In … dontstopdontstopdontstopdontstop, edited by April Elizabeth Lamm, 21–23. London: Sternberg, 2006.

61. Scott, Carrie. "In Your Face: Hans Ulrich Obrist." SHOWStudio, December 5, 2014. Video, 48:21. https://www.youtube.com/watch?v=t0GYVY9i28Q.

62. Obrist, Hans Ulrich, and Ingo Niermann. "The Elephant Trunk in Dubai." In *Everything You Wanted to Know about Curating* *But Were Afraid to Ask*, edited by April Lamm, 31–57. London: Sternberg, 2011.

63. Obrist, Hans Ulrich, and Brendan McGetrick. "A Mad Dinner in Reagan's War Room." In *Everything You Wanted to Know about Curating* *But Were Afraid to Ask*, edited by April Lamm, 69–83. 3. London: Sternberg, 2011.

64. Obrist, Hans Ulrich, and Jefferson Hack. "The Enemies Are Those Audio Guides." In *Everything You Wanted to Know about*

Curating* *But Were Afraid to Ask, edited by April Lamm,
85–93. London: Sternberg, 2011.

65. Obrist, Hans Ulrich, and Markus Miessen. "The Importance of Being in the Kitchen." In Everything You Wanted to Know about Curating* *But Were Afraid to Ask, edited by April Lamm, 117–22. London: Sternberg, 2011.

66. Obrist, Hans Ulrich, and Gavin Wade. "A Protest against Forgetting." In Everything You Wanted to Know about Curating* *But Were Afraid to Ask, edited by April Lamm, 123–42. London: Sternberg, 2011.

67. Obrist, Hans Ulrich, and Noah Horowitz. "Can Exhibitions Be Collected?" In Everything You Wanted to Know about Curating* *But Were Afraid to Ask, edited by April Lamm, 143–64. London: Sternberg, 2011.

68. Obrist, Hans Ulrich, and Paul O'Neill. "It's Alive." In Everything You Wanted to Know about Curating* *But Were Afraid to Ask, edited by April Lamm, 175–84. London: Sternberg, 2011.

69. Obrist, Hans Ulrich, and Jean-Max Colard. "Labomatic." In Everything You Wanted to Know about Curating* *But Were Afraid to Ask, edited by April Lamm, 185–96. London: Sternberg, 2011.

70. Obrist, Hans Ulrich. "The Tree Shelter." Plant 11 (2017): 20–22.

71. Obrist, Hans Ulrich, and Enrique Walker. "Before and

After." In *Everything You Wanted to Know about Curating* *But Were Afraid to Ask*, edited by April Lamm, 15–20. London: Sternberg, 2011.

72. "Always the Beginning: Hans Ulrich Obrist on Hans Ulrich Obrist." Unpublished, 2016.

73. Obrist, Hans Ulrich. *Ways of Curating*. New York: Farrar, Straus and Giroux, 2014.

74. Obrist, Hans Ulrich. *Sharp Tongues, Loose Lips, Open Eyes, Ears to the Ground*. London: Sternberg, 2014.

75. Obrist, Hans Ulrich. *Somewhere Totally Else*. Geneva: JRP | Ringier, 2018.

76. Obrist, Hans Ulrich. "TAKE ME (I'M YOURS)." Unpublished draft of *Ways of Curating*.

77. Obrist, Hans Ulrich. Preface to *Envision 2116*. Edited by Hans Ulrich Obrist and Yongwoo Lee. Shanghai: Shanghai Himalayas Museum, 2016.

78. Obrist, Hans Ulrich. Preface to *Worldbuilding Exhibition Booklet*. Julia Stoschek Foundation, June 2022. https://www.jsfoundation.art/wpcontent/uploads/2022/05/WORLDBUILDING_Booklet.pdf.

79. Obrist, Hans Ulrich. "Journey of a Young Swiss Man." In *David Weiss: Works, 1968–1979*, edited by Karen Marta and Simon Castets, 207–15. New York: Swiss Institute, 2016.

80. Obrist, Hans Ulrich. "Stuttgart-London Interview Marathons." Unpublished, 2004.

81. Alecega, Nicolas Delgado. "On Encounters, Constructing Reality, and Listening." *Pairs* 1 (Spring 2021).

82. Obrist, Hans Ulrich. "Michel Serres in Conversation with Hans Ulrich Obrist." Unpublished, 2017.

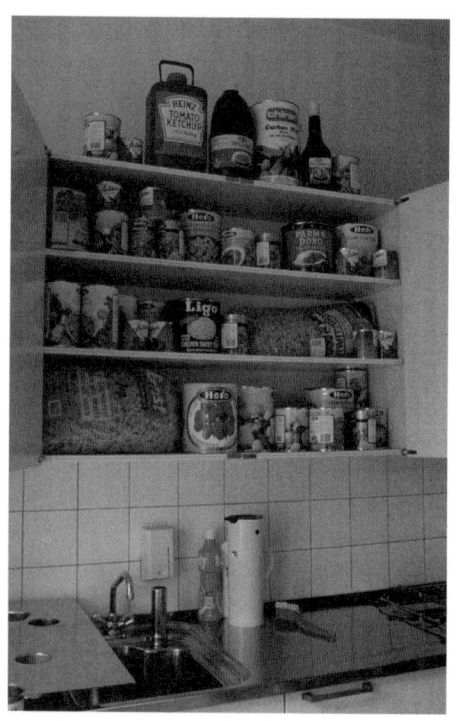

CHRONOLOGY

Throughout his career, Hans Ulrich Obrist has curated 350 exhibitions and published over 500 catalogs and titles. For brevity, only a selection is highlighted here.

1968
Hans Ulrich Obrist is born in Zurich, Switzerland.

1987
He enrolls at the University of St. Gallen, studying
  economics.

1991
Obrist organizes his first exhibition, *World Soup (The
  Kitchen Show)*, in the kitchen of his St. Gallen apart-
  ment, challenging traditional exhibition spaces.
  He becomes curator in residence at the Cartier
  Foundation in Paris.

1993

Obrist curates the Do It series, inspired by a conversation
with artists Christian Boltanski and Bertrand Lavier.
The series invites artists to contribute "instructions"
that can be reinterpreted with each enactment. Since
its inauguration, Do It has been presented in more
than fifty location worldwide.

1993–96

He establishes the "Migrateurs" program at the Musée
d'Art Moderne de la Ville de Paris, featuring thirty
exhibitions by individual artists engaging with the
museum's space.

1993–2000

Obrist serves as curator for the museum in progress art
association in Vienna and lectures at the Leuphana
University of Lüneburg.

1995

Obrist cocurates *Take Me (I'm Yours)* at the Serpentine
    Gallery in London. The innovative exhibition invites
    audiences to interact with and even take home the
    objects, redefining the relationship between artist,
    object, and viewer. Iterations of the exhibition are
    later presented in Paris, New York, Milan, and in
    2014, the Swiss Pavilion at the fourteenth Interna-
    tional Architecture Biennale in Venice.

1997–

He founds and becomes editor in chief of the magazine
    Point d'Ironie, published by fashion designer agnès b.

1996–2000

Obrist cocurates *Cities on the Move*, a major exhibition
    addressing urbanization in East and Southeast Asia
    in the late twentieth century. Featuring more than
    150 artists, architects, filmmakers, and designers, the
    project travels to ten sites worldwide, reinventing
    itself with each iteration.

1999

He cocurates *Laboratorium*, an interdisciplinary exhibition in Antwerp, Belgium, that questions the role of studios and laboratories as spaces for artistic and scientific production.

2000–2006

Obrist is a curator at the Musée d'Art Moderne de la Ville de Paris.

2006–

He is appointed codirector of exhibitions and programs as well as director of international projects at the Serpentine Galleries in London—a position he continues to hold.

2007

Obrist cocurates the operatic group exhibition *Il Tempo del Postino* with artist Philippe Parreno at the Manchester International Festival (MIF). Rather than presenting a group of physical works that the audience can navigate at its own pace, the exhibition presents a sequence of performances and time-based artworks on stage. He also publishes the first volume in *The Conversation Series*, a project born out of the thousands of hours of interviews that he continues to conduct, which he calls "an endless conversation." To date, twenty-eight titles in the series have been released.

2008

Obrist publishes *A Brief History of Curating*, part of the Documents series created by nonprofit Swiss art publishers JRP Editions.

2009

Il Tempo del Postino is presented in Basel, Switzerland. Obrist is ranked number one in *ArtReview* magazine's annual list of the art world's hundred most important people. He is also awarded an honorary fellowship by the Royal Institute of British Architects.

2011

Obrist receives the CCS Bard Award for Curatorial
    Excellence.

2011–15

He cocurates 11 *Rooms*, a time-based group exhibition
    that travels to four additional venues, renaming it 12,
    13, 14, and 15 *Rooms* in each new location.

2013–

The Handwriting Project, protesting the disappearance of
    handwriting in the digital age, launches on Instagram
    (@hansulrichobrist).

2014

Obrist publishes *Ways of Curating*, a distillation of his
    years of experience in the art world.

2015

He writes *The Age of Earthquakes* with Douglas Coupland
    and Shumon Basar, and *Lives of the Artists, Lives of Ar-*

chitects. Obrist is awarded the International Folkwang Prize too, acknowledging outstanding individuals in the promotion and communication of art.

2016
He is once again ranked number one in *ArtReview* magazine's annual Power 100 list.

2018
Obrist receives the Appraisers Association of America Award for Excellence in the Arts.

2020
Obrist curates *Enzo Mari*, a major retrospective at Triennale Milano honoring one of Italy's most important artists.

2021
He publishes three books: *The Extreme Self: Age of You*, *140 Ideas for Planet Earth*, and *Édouard Glissant: Archipelago*.

2022

Obrist curates *WORLDBUILDING: Gaming and Art in the Digital Age* at the Julia Stoschek Collection in Dusseldorf, Germany. The exhibition explores the relationship between video games and digital art, showcasing how artists have reacted to and integrated this mass phenomenon into their work.

2023

WORLDBUILDING is presented at the Centre Pompidou-Metz. Obrist also publishes *James Lovelock: Ever Gaia, Remember to Dream*, and *Une vie in Progress*.

2024

Obrist publishes *Gustav Metzger: Interviews with Hans Ulrich Obrist*.

ACKNOWLEDGMENTS

To Hans Ulrich, my heartfelt gratitude for sharing your words and thoughts in this publication. Your boundless creativity, vision, and ability to foster connection continue to inspire me.

My deepest thanks also goes to Max Shackleton, Lorraine Testro Two, and Adele Koechlin whose meticulous archival work and dedication has been essential in the production of this publication.

I am profoundly thankful to the entire team at Princeton University Press for its unwavering dedication and support. My special thanks to Michelle Komie, Christie Henry, Terri O'Prey, Cindy Milstein, Jacqueline Poirier, Colleen Suljic, Laurie Schlesinger, Cathy Felgar, Jodi Price, Kathryn Stevens, Annie Miller, William Skurka, and Alexandria Leonard. Your professionalism and passion have been instrumental in bringing our projects to life over the years.

Heartfelt thanks as well to Mike Dean and Louise Donegan.

Special appreciation also goes to editorial director Fiona Graham, whose leadership has guided this project and the entire ISMs series. My thanks as well to Susan Delson for her insightful editorial contributions and Vanessa Lee for her early research assistance.

My sincere thanks, too, to Taliesin Thomas and Steven Rodríguez for their ongoing support.

Above all, I give all of my bottomless gratitude to my amazing wife, Abbey, and my wonderful children, Justin, Ethan, Ellie, and Jonah, for their love and encouragement.

As always, I give endless love and thanks to my mother, Judith.

LARRY WARSH
JANUARY 2025

Hans Ulrich Obrist (b. 1968, Zurich, Switzerland) is the artistic director of Serpentine in London and senior adviser at LUMA Arles. Prior to this, he was the curator of the Musée d'Art Moderne de la Ville de Paris. Since his first show, *World Soup (The Kitchen Show)*, in 1991, he has curated more than 350 exhibitions, including recent exhibitions *Enzo Mari* at Triennale Milano (2020) as well as *WORLDBUILDING* at Centre Pompidou Metz (2023) and Julia Stoschek Collection Dusseldorf (2022).

In 2011, Obrist received the CCS Bard Award for Curatorial Excellence, and in 2015, he was awarded the International Folkwang Prize. Most recently, he was honored by the Appraisers Association of America with the 2018 Award for Excellence in the Arts. Obrist's recent publications include *Ways of Curating* (2015), *The Age of Earthquakes* (2015), *Lives of the Artists, Lives of Architects* (2015), *The Extreme Self: Age of You* (2021), *140 Ideas for Planet Earth* (2021), *Edouard Glissant: Archipelago* (2021), *James Lovelock: Ever Gaia* (2023), *Remember to Dream* (2023), and *Une vie in Progress* (2023).

Larry Warsh has been active in the art world for more than thirty years as a publisher and artist-collaborator. An early collector of Keith Haring and Jean-Michel Basquiat, Warsh was a lead organizer for the exhibition *Basquiat: The Unknown Notebooks*, which debuted at the Brooklyn Museum, New York, in 2015, and later traveled to several US museums. He has loaned artworks by Haring and Basquiat from his collection to numerous exhibitions worldwide, and served as a curatorial consultant on *Keith Haring | Jean-Michel Basquiat: Crossing Lines* for the National Gallery of Victoria.

The founder of *Museums Magazine*, Warsh has been involved in many publishing projects, and is the editor of the -isms series and several other titles published by Princeton University Press, including *Jean-Michel Basquiat's The Notebooks* (2017), *Keith Haring: 31 Subway Drawings* (2021), and two books by Ai Weiwei, *Humanity* (2018) and *Weiwei-isms* (2012).

Warsh has served on the board of the Getty Museum Photographs Council and was a founding member of the Basquiat Authentication Committee until its dissolution in 2012.

ILLUSTRATIONS

Frontispiece: Portrait of Hans Ulrich Obrist by Lukas Wassmann.

Page 142: Fischli/Weiss, *The Kitchen Show*, curated by Hans Ulrich Obrist, 1991.

ISMs

Larry Warsh, Series Editor

The ISMs series distills the voices of an exciting range of visual artists and designers into captivating, beautifully made books of quotations for a new generation of readers. In turn passionate, inspiring, humorous, witty, and challenging, these collections offer powerful statements on topics ranging from contemporary culture, politics, and race, to creativity, humanity, and the role of art in the world. Books in this series are edited by Larry Warsh and published by Princeton University Press in association with No More Rulers.

Calder-isms, Alexander Calder

Obrist-isms, Hans Ulrich Obrist

Ono-isms, Yoko Ono

Minter-isms, Marilyn Minter

Fairey-isms, Shepard Fairey

Abramović-isms, Marina Abramović

JR-isms, JR

Holzer-isms: Artist's Edition, Jenny Holzer

Neshat-isms, Shirin Neshat

Judy Chicago-isms, Judy Chicago

Pharrell-isms, Pharrell Williams

Hirst-isms, Damien Hirst

Warhol-isms, Andy Warhol

Arsham-isms, Daniel Arsham

Abloh-isms, Virgil Abloh

Futura-isms, Futura

Haring-isms, Keith Haring

Basquiat-isms, Jean-Michel Basquiat